Manor Houses of Bedfordshire

Past and Present

David Villanueva

DEDICATION

To Helen

CONTENTS

ACKNOWLEDGMENTS

Several images are reused in this book, with grateful thanks, under various Creative Commons Licences. To view copies of these licences, visit http://creativecommons.org/licenses/ or send a letter to Creative Commons, 171 Second Street, Suite 300, San Francisco, California, 94105, USA.

A few aerial images have been used with grateful thanks to Google and their partners. Thanks also to all who have so generously made their work freely available online at Wikipedia.org and elsewhere.

1 INTRODUCTION

Whether they ever functioned as a Manor, Bedfordshire boasts an impressive display of many country Mansions; homes of nobility and gentry, built at vast expense, presenting a rich variety of architecture surrounded by landscaped gardens. But before we look at specific Manor Houses, and their history up to the present day it is worthwhile to explore the general history of such Mansions in Britain.

No trace stands above ground of Ancient British round houses as these were simple wooden structures, not built to last. Sites relatively quickly became contaminated, causing moving and rebuilding afresh. The Romans introduced refinements and our ancestors gained a regular, ornamental, and durable style of architecture. The Romano-British, who remained after the legions left, inherited Roman civilisation and all early architecture remaining has the Roman style but degrades over time until superseded by Saxon building.

The Saxons were farmers and built functional houses with no great adornment. The frequent and harassing Viking raids not only retarded the progress of architecture, but contributed to the destruction of many fine examples. Alfred the Great (c.848-899) revived the arts and excelled his predecessors in building elegance and in the adornments of his palaces.

The Norman Conquest (1066) brought the arts from a comparatively enlightened people. They were a nation fond of state and military grandeur. They introduced the Feudal system, requiring a Castle to every large estate. The Normans acquired the property from the Saxons and spared no cost in erecting grand and secure buildings on their various Baronies. Castles were constructed primarily for defence. Of the few which remain inhabited, the walls only resemble the ancient Baronial residence; customs and manners have materially changed, to the extent that a castle with its original rooms would now be uninhabitable. The walls were several feet thick, and towers of various heights appeared at the numerous angles. In the centre was the large Keep; the surrounding area divided into courts was used for war games played out by the Baron, his Knights, and Esquires. Within these Baronial Fortresses the ancient landed Lords displayed their hospitality and courtesy to their connections and retainers. The children of their superior vassals received their education.

Plan of a medieval Manor, from William R Shepherd, *Historical Atlas*

The Feudal System, instilled a high sense of honour and military pride but admitted only two ranks of society, the Barons and their vassals, who were chiefly employed in cultivating the Manor lands which they held under tenure. The only trade then carried on was through periodical fairs, but society was gradually improving by the introduction of commerce.

The great chiefs were almost continually engaged in warfare, which destroyed many of the ancient nobility and simultaneously brought about a great change in landed property. Henry VII won the crown in 1485 ending the Wars of the Roses. He banned private armies, which lessened the Barons' grandeur. The younger branches of many noble families embraced the opportunity afforded by trade to increase their inheritance. The King's political motives encouraged Commerce and created a new class of subjects, balancing the power of the nobles and producing a more equal distribution of wealth, much of which was liberally applied to the decoration of recently erected Mansions.

From the events of Henry VII's reign (1485-1509) originated a new architecture, although we rarely find examples in their original form. The same plan continued in the following reign of Henry VIII (1509-47), calculated to display much hospitality, later made more necessary by the dissolution of the monasteries, where formerly travellers were entertained, and the poor provided with food. Such folk now turned to the Mansions of the nobility, for that support which was sometimes made a condition in the grants of ecclesiastical property. Magnitude was a necessary character of these buildings, which presented an air of seclusion with all the main windows looking into the Quadrangle which the building surrounded. The larger Baronial Mansions showed two of these open Courts: the first containing the lodgings of the household officers; the second, the principal and state chambers, with the hall and chapel.

These buildings were mostly constructed of brick, some faced with fine black flints, and ornamented in chequered and other varied forms; dates, and even names, have been so produced. The quoins, cornices, and other dressings were of stone. The principal decoration of the exterior was at the grand entrance, which usually exhibited ostentatious heraldic devices.

Among the accessories to the main building, besides the Stables and Kennel for the hounds, was the Mews or Falconry, for hawks. It was also customary to have large ponds nearby for the breeding and preserving of fish, which made up essential food; and when the Roman Catholic religion prevailed, were required in great abundance.

Most of the very sumptuous Houses erected in the reign of Henry VIII are now either lost, dilapidated, or modernized. Hengrave Hall, Suffolk is a magnificent exception.

When Henry VIII dissolved the monasteries, many of the King's favourites received noble Manors and large estates that had belonged to the dissolved houses. The monastic buildings furnished materials for new Mansions; as with Chicksands Priory, in Bedfordshire. Of the architects employed in this reign, we only know the names of a few. In the erection of part of the Palace of Whitehall, Henry supposedly used the designs of the celebrated Hans Holbein the Younger (1497-1543). John of Padua (active 1543-57), an Italian, is in some deeds termed "devisor of his Majestie's buildings".

The plans of these noble quadrangular buildings were similar; they comprised an extensive range of apartments, which would be unnecessary today. The Baronial Mansion's Great Hall was dedicated to hospitality and pomp. Notable for its large size, it generally occupied one side of the quadrangle or open court; it stood the height of the building, having an open-worked timber roof, enriched with ornaments, chosen from the heraldic insignia of the family, producing a grand effect. The Great Halls are all that remain of Westminster and Eltham Palaces.

These Mansions were conveniently adapted for the immense establishments supported by the nobility of the 16th century. The Earl of Northumberland, one of the most powerful barons of the time, retained two hundred and twenty-three staff and Thomas, Earl of Dorset, had in his family a little less than two hundred.

The gradual change, from increasing commerce caused a progressive alteration in the economy among the great. Country residences became more numerous, but less extensive in their plan; more comfortable and less splendid and ostentatious.

In the reigns of Queen Elizabeth I (1558-1603) and James I (1603-25), Italian, French, and Flemish architects were occasionally employed in Britain. Classic architecture initially became evident in fantastic ornaments, originally mingled with the ancient style of building. These comprised elaborate panels, balustrades, small statues and later, columns and pilasters covered with netlike ornamentation. Terminals, sculptured brackets, and draped female figure support pillars were also used on the large chimney pieces inside and at the external porch and centre compartment of the Front. Blickling Hall, Norfolk is an excellent example. Medallions and busts of the twelve Caesars were also frequently introduced, at this time, together with pyramids, globes, obelisks, and allegorical devices, intermixed with shields of arms and family crests.

A particular style of garden developed around the chief Mansions. No original garden remains, but there are several recreations such as at Kenilworth Castle in Warwickshire.

Longleat in Wiltshire, the home of the Marquess of Bath, is the earliest specimen of classical architecture in Britain. It was completed in 1579, on designs from Italy by John Thorpe (1565-1655). Audley End, Essex, was built between 1603 and 1616, by Bernard Jansen, a Flemish architect of great repute; but on an Italian model. John Smithson, a British architect, was sent to Italy by the Earl of Newcastle, to collect designs for improvements to the now ruined Bolsover Castle, in Derbyshire, began in 1613.

Architecture had matured in Greece. The Doric order, the most ancient and pure; the Ionic, distinguished by its spiral scrolls; and the Corinthian, having its capital adorned with acanthus leaves were each named after the people who invented them. The Romans modified and adopted these orders in their buildings. The Romans added the Tuscan order, from Tuscany, Italy and the Composite: the first derived from the Doric, the last from an union of the Corinthian and Ionic. These form the five orders of the Roman architect, Vitruvius, whose architecture peaked in the reign of Emperor Augustus, (63BC -14AD) who boasted that he had found Rome of brick and left it of marble. The science prevailed for the next 200 years, then went into decline and with the fall of the Western Empire it sunk into obscurity.

In Italy, a revival began in the 15th century under the auspices of the Medici family. The architect of the Palazzo Pitti, at Florence, Leon Battista Alberti, was the first to restore classic taste. He was called the modern Vitruvius from his writings on the subject. Michelangelo (1475-1564) attained the theory of ancient art by careful admeasurements of antique remains and contributed his comprehensive genius to revive ancient architecture. But the great genius of modern Italy, whose rules were liberally adopted in Britain, was Andrea Palladio (1508-80), from Lombardy: forming his designs entirely on ancient models, he gained great simplicity and purity of taste. His superior claim to elegant and graceful design was readily acknowledged by his contemporaries who extolled him as the unequalled Raphael of Architects. The Palladian Style continued to retain its attractions into the early 20th century.

One beautiful design of Palladio's, that of the Villa Capra near his native town of Vicenza, has always been justly admired for the exquisite harmony reigning over every part of the building. This has been frequently adopted in England, as a model of superior taste but always on a smaller scale, as at the celebrated Chiswick House, London built by Richard Boyle, 3rd earl of Burlington, (1694-1753), an English architect and one originator of the English Palladian or Neo-Palladian style of the 18th century.

Inigo Jones (1573-1652) born in London. As an apprentice joiner he first gained an accurate knowledge of the mechanical part of his profession. His superior talents attracted the attention of a generous patron of the arts, Thomas Howard, Earl of Arundel, at whose expense he explored Italy, and enriched his mind studying its architectural treasures. Christian IV invited him to Denmark and as soon as he arrived, he was appointed Architect to James I's Queen, sister of the King of Denmark. In this capacity he rebuilt the waterfront of the Queen's residence at Somerset House, then called Denmark House. This Facade by Jones was notable as the first pure design erected in England, formed upon the antique. It has since been demolished but many views of it remain.

Inigo Jones visited Italy a second time to further improve his profession. Regrettably, his design masterpiece, the Royal Palace at Whitehall; a building originally conceived upon a scale so magnificent, that it would have been as splendid as the Louvre, was never completed. The ground plan, an immense parallelogram, 1153 feet long, by 874 feet deep, having its extreme length east and west, extended over the space between the river Thames, and St. James's Park, fronting Charing Cross and the city of Westminster. It included seven courts, the largest in the centre, and three on each side. The only part erected was the Banqueting House, intended for the reception of foreign ambassadors, which was built in 1619. This portion of the intended Palace comprises three stories: the first rusticated, the second has Ionic columns and the third of the Composite Order. It was completed at a cost of £15,618. From the designs of this Palace, we can estimate the abilities of the architect, whose genius effected a complete change in our domestic buildings.

The distracted state of the nation which followed the accession of Charles I (1625-49) prevented the completion of the Palace; but established a confirmed taste for the genuine antique which completely superseded the mixed and extravagant style, adopted chiefly from the Flemish and early Italian architects during the reigns of Elizabeth I and James I.

Inigo Jones died in 1651 but during his lifetime, he built or modified more than a dozen country Houses. Many of these have been totally destroyed, and others altered beyond recognition, although various views of the originals survive. It was not only the elevation that underwent a total change but the ground plan varied alike. The enclosed quadrangle, or later half H, were generally discarded for a more compact plan, widely differing from that of the ancient Mansion originally borrowed from the monastery. The elevation was now endowed with a stately portico having the tympanum filled with heraldic arms. The new design excluded the Great Hall, but replaced it with an entrance hall, based on the Italian Sola for communication with different suites of rooms. The sashed frame replaced the mullioned window with its small panes of coloured glass, allowing views over the raised terrace surrounding the building and the countryside beyond.

The Civil War (1642-51) and its aftermath retarded the useful progress of art; and it was not until after the Restoration that any considerable advances were made in classical design.

The Restoration of Charles II (1660-85) brought back royalty, not taste. All art appears to have been derived from France; Mansions, gardens, statues, pictures, etc. Nothing opposed the splendour seen at the court of Louis XIV, we readily accepted the most basic imitations. The greatest architect of his time went no further than Paris to complete his studies. Fortunately, native British genius prevailed and in the works of Sir Christopher Wren (1632-1723), there is less of the exuberant French school, than in the buildings of his contemporaries and his immediate followers. Hampton Court Palace, which he altered, is almost the only Mansion in which his hand appears. The elevations of that building are magnificent. In gardening and planting, we employed French artists owing to a shortage in the profession at home. The avenues of trees planted at given distances, the long straight walk and canal, are all of French origin. As also are the geometrically formed parterres, topiary and waterworks of every description. Statues were considered indispensable in forming a perfect garden, from a single figure to the complete group.

The finest example of a noble House in England, erected along these lines, is Chatsworth in Derbyshire. Caius Gabriel Cibber (1630-1700), a Dane, was much patronized by William, Duke of Devonshire, and produced most of the statues which abound there.

The profusely ornamental style of the gardens at Chatsworth are probably the best remaining example. But Gardens soon lost the air of Italian grace and French liveliness. On the accession of William III (1688-1702), British nobility obtained their ideas of pastoral beauty from Holland, and their rural Houses, became surrounded by a space levelled dead flat and divided by Canals. Uneven ground was converted into a terrace ascended by stone steps, broad gravel walks were planted with ranges of trees or impenetrable hedges of holly and yew. A high wall was built around the garden or park. The façade of the Mansion was usually built of red brick relieved by an equal distribution of stone. The high roof with two or more tiers of dormer windows rose from a heavy projecting cornice which replaced the balustrade. Dalkeith Palace in Midlothian, Scotland, was modeled on a Palace of the Princes of Orange, at Het Loo, in the Netherlands.

In the Reign of Queen Anne (1702-14), although little advancement was made in design, love of splendor and magnificence prevailed in the Noble Mansions of that period. Blenheim, in Oxfordshire, was erected at public expense, in gratitude, for military services rendered by the Duke of Marlborough. James Brydges, whose ostentatious ideas earned him, the nickname of "The Grand" Duke of Chandos built its grand rival, Cannons House in Middlesex. Following the death of the Duke, in 1744, his son and heir could not afford to maintain the House and demolished it in 1747. Other Mansions almost equally splendid, albeit on a smaller scale followed its fate; such as Eastbury, in Dorset and Wricklemarsh House at Blackheath: their rapid downfall were the effects of new families rashly emulating the excesses of the ancient barons. While Petworth House, in Sussex, Heythrop, in Oxfordshire, Castle Howard and Bramham Park, both in Yorkshire remain proud examples of an age of magnificent architecture.

In the commencement of the 18th century, the British architects whose superb designs deservedly placed them at the head of their profession, were Sir John Vanbrugh (1664-1726) and James Gibbs (1682-1752) who studied the first principles of his art in Rome. The most celebrated buildings by Vanbrugh, are Blenheim (Oxon), Castle Howard (Yorks), Duncombe Park (Yorks), Grimsthorpe (Lincs), Kings Weston (Bristol), and Seaton Delaval (Northumberland). Gibbs erected Ditchley, in Oxfordshire. These Mansions are all grandly and boldly constructed but lack purity of outline and are excessively ornamented. Thomas Ripley (1682-1758) and Colen Campbell (1676-1729) who followed, were both highly celebrated in their day, and were succeeded by Sir Robert Taylor (1714–1788) and James Paine (1717–1789). Ripley designed Houghton Hall and Wolterton Hall, both in Norfolk. Campbell built Mereworth in Kent; Sir Robert Taylor designed Heveningham Hall in Suffolk and Gorhambury in Hertfordshire and James Paine was the architect responsible for New Wardour Castle in Wiltshire, Worksop Manor in Nottinghamshire, and Thorndon Hall in Essex. Observing their work shows that the building elevations were gradually relieved of decorations in use during the early part of the century. The Adam brothers entirely discarded heavy cornices, rusticated quoins and columns, forming their designs on a survey of the palace of the Emperor

Diocletian, at Split in Croatia. The finest specimens of the architecture of the brothers, Robert Adam (1728-1792) and James Adam (1732–1794), are Luton Hoo, in Bedfordshire, Kedleston in Derbyshire, Compton Verney in Warwickshire, and Kenwood House in Middlesex. James 'Athenian' Stuart (1713–1788) was the first of his profession who studied and took exact measurements of the principal existing Temples in Greece and established the foundation of a decided taste for elegance in architecture. Correct models, erected by him, adorn the Grounds at Shugborough in Staffordshire.

James Wyatt (1746-1813) started a revival of the neglected beauty of Gothic architecture. The splendid Mansion at Ashridge in Hertfordshire attests to the progress he had made in restoring the style of Baronial Residences. Neo-Gothic architecture is evident at Donington Hall in Leicestershire, Eaton Hall in Cheshire, Tregothnan in Cornwall, Eastnor Castle in Herefordshire and many others.

The most remarkable transition occurred during the 18th century in the extensive and diversified parks and beautiful gardens of country residences, where landscapes blended in with the countryside. William Kent (1685-1748), under the patronage of the Earl of Burlington, introduced a more natural look, planting hills with clumps and turning the extended view to advantage, while concealing any partial defects. He is justly considered the inventor of modern landscape gardening. His pupil and successor was the celebrated Launcelot Brown (1715-83), whose constant use of the word earned him the epithet of Capability. Under his direction and practical experience, he carried ornamental gardening to high perfection at many places for nearly half a century such as at Luton in Bedfordshire and Blenheim in Oxfordshire. Among Brown's contemporaries were Charles Hamilton (1704-86) who created Painshill, in Surrey, progressing a purely natural and varied disposition of decorated scenery. Valentine Morris (1727-89) was the sole director of the improvements made in the once beautiful and well-known gardens at Piercefield, near Chepstow. Humphry Repton (1752–1818) often regarded as Brown's successor and the last great landscape designer of the 18th century, designed gardens at Moggerhanger House and Woburn Abbey in Bedfordshire.

The building, enlarging and remodelling of country Houses continued through the 19th century, but by the end of the century, problems arose for some Houses and their owners. In 1894, the government introduced death duties and taxation rose during the 20th century. For some landowners, Manor Houses were becoming too large and expensive to live in. World War I created a labour shortage with a consequent rise in wages, and domestic staff became increasingly difficult and expensive to obtain. During World War II, the military requisitioned and damaged many Houses so much that post-war compensation was inadequate to cover the costs of repairs. Since 1900, some 20% of English Manor Houses have been demolished, but that means that 80% have survived and barring major disasters should continue to do so. Not so many Manor Houses these days are the homes of a single aristocratic family, but many have survived through the National Trust; as corporate or organizational buildings or redesigned as residential apartments.

This is the story of the main Manor Houses of Bedfordshire…

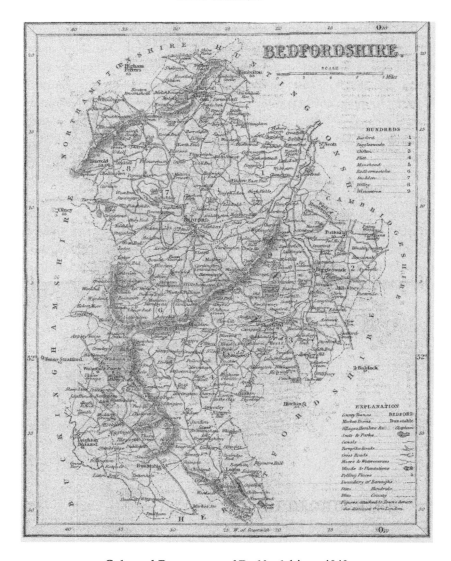

Cole and Roper map of Bedfordshire c.1840

2 IN SEARCH OF LOST MANOR HOUSES

I did not particularly write this book for metal detectorists and archaeologists, however since Manor Houses represented the wealth of Britain there is a great interest in searching the sites of former Manors, since they frequently produce high quality coins and artefacts. Such properties were featured frequently in Channel 4's former *Time Team* programs.

I can illustrate my point with two garden searches I made a few years ago. The first was that of a town house built some 70 years previously, with a reasonably generous garden amounting to two hundred square yards. In that garden, I found over fifty coins and a finger ring. The 20th century ring would originally have been handsome, replete with gilding and possibly a real imitation diamond in its central cavity. However, every single find was base metal, not a scrap of silver nor hint of gold.

In contrast, I was involved in a metal detecting club search in the grounds of a Manor House built some 700 years previously, with a very generous garden of about nine acres. Although 18 of us only searched for four hours, we found well over fifty coins and artefacts, several of which were silver. In addition, I made one gold find here, a Tudor iconographic finger ring. The coroner subsequently declared the ring treasure, and it now resides in Canterbury Museum.

Gold Tudor finger ring showing saints Catherine and John the Baptist

This particular Manor House was not lost, of course, but there are literally thousands of former Manor Houses and associated parks throughout the country, which have disappeared. Many former Manors are now mainly accessible farmland. So how does something as large as a Manor House become lost? One of the main reasons seems to be destruction by fire. Another is the family outgrew the House and rebuilt nearby. Often the House was surplus to requirements, the family having gained other Houses by marriage or inheritance. Whatever the reason for the House being abandoned, the buildings often disappeared because valuable building materials were reused elsewhere.

How then do you find the sites of Manor Houses if the buildings are no longer standing? The short answer is to study local history books and maps. One thing that early local history writers and map makers quickly learned was that the wealthy and worthies almost invariably bought the books and maps. Including details of such families and their Houses in the texts and images, guaranteed sales.

If you want to find lost Manors, start with an old county map showing Manors (often referred to as seats) and parks. Your local library will have a range of maps and will know where you can find others. You can even buy reprints of many notable county maps if you want your own copy. Computer users will find a large range of county maps at Genmaps. You can go back as far as the 17th century with maps by John Speed, for instance, and then work forward checking against maps through the 18th and 19th centuries. Note all Manorial parks in your area of interest and if and when they appear and disappear.

Once you have found a few Manors of interest, you should be able to get some historical information by consulting the major county history for your area. If you browse any county history book published around 1800, it reads like a who's who of the local gentry, detailing their lands and Houses. You will probably be surprised by what you find in these old accounts, which eye-witnesses wrote in many cases. The information will also come in handy to show the landowner when seeking permission.

Sometimes you will get a precise location of a lost Manor from the county history but if not, you can study old and more recent Ordnance Survey maps. The early 19th century one inch first series (reprints available) will show Manors existing then, while later maps will show Manors remaining and the sites of those lost since the first series. Larger scale Ordnance Survey maps, produced after 1850, will show greater detail, but be aware that many antiquities have been removed from very recent Ordnance Survey maps. The two-and-a-half inch Pathfinder series, for instance, shows many more antiquities than the Explorer series, which replaced it in 2003.

While the Manor House may have disappeared, often it is still remembered in a remaining feature or a name, such as fishponds, dovecote, moat, ice house, gatehouse, lodge, chapel or park. It is common for the Manor name to have been given to a building or wood or recorded as a field name on a tithe map. If a fire destroyed a Manor House, the name Burnt House is a reliable clue to the event.

I have had the good fortune of being able to search four lost Manor sites, with a metal detector and every one has produced a wealth of finds.

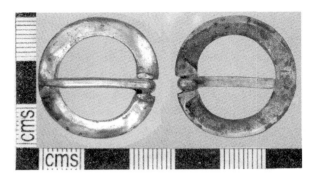

13th-14th century silver annular brooch

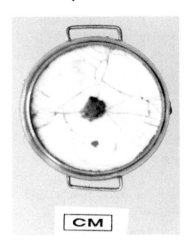

1920s gold wristwatch

16th century silver hooked clothing fastener

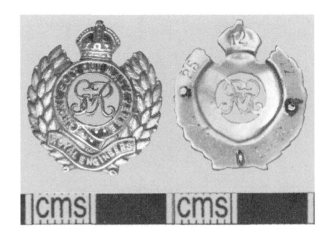

World War I gold sweetheart brooch

Edward III gold quarter noble coin, 1346-77

3 AMPTHILL PARK

Ampthill Park c.1820

In the 13th century and probably earlier, the Baronial family of Poinz held this Manor. In 1218, Henry III (1216-72) granted a licence for a market to Nicholas Poinz, and Joan, his wife, every Tuesday at their Manor of Ampthill. The Estate is located in a valley in Redbornestoke Hundred and is about a quarter of a mile northeast of Ampthill market town.

Ampthill Park was a Royal Lodge and hunting Park from the 14th century. Early in the 15th century Henry IV (1399-1413) gave the Manor to his brother-in-law Sir John Cornwall, Lord Fanhope, who had married Elizabeth of Lancaster, Duchess of Exeter, the King's sister. He built a large fortified House on this Estate, called Ampthill Castle. The Estate reverted to the crown and Edward IV (1461-83) granted it to Edmund, Lord Grey, of Ruthin, later Earl of Kent. Richard, 3rd Earl of Kent, his grandson, squandered his inheritance, and the Mansion was handed over to Henry VIII, (1509-47) becoming his Palace and hunting Lodge. Queen Katharine of Aragon lived there for two years during the time of her divorce. There is a plan of this Castle, drawn about 1619. The Castle was demolished soon after.

In 1661, Charles II (1660-85) granted the Manor to John Ashburnham, who was created Lord Ashburnham in 1698. He built the present House of red brick to the north of the Castle site. About 1720 Richard, Viscount Fitzwilliam bought the House and Estate and in 1736, it was sold to Anne, Lady Gowran, the grandmother of the Earl of Upper Ossory.

The Earl of Upper Ossory, remodelled the House in classical style: the building was encased with a composition resembling stone. The arms of Fitz Patrick were carved above the porch on the main front and a bust placed over the door; two flights of steps were added to the entrance. The engraving shows the House little changed from then. The Earl of Upper Ossory died in 1818, aged 72, and left this Estate to Lord Holland, whose mother, Lady Mary Fitz Patrick, was the late Earl's sister.

The army occupied the Estate during World War II. Volunteers at a farming camp near Ampthill, harvested sugar beet and were housed in tents in the grounds. The park was opened to the public following the War and Bovril Ltd bought the House, which became a Cheshire Home for the Disabled in 1955. In 1979, the grade II listed Mansion was converted into four large residential dwellings. The Park is listed grade II.

4 APSLEY HOUSE OR SHILLINGTON MANOR

1 Shillington Manor; 2 Apsley Bury Farm moated site; 3 Moat. Map data: copyright 2018 The GeoInformation Group, Infoterra Ltd & Bluesky, Google

The Victorian county map shows Apsley House and a small Park at Apsley End. Apsley House is now called Shillington Manor and was once Apsley Bury Manor. Apsley Bury Farm, a short distance north, has evidence of a moat and further north, just before the village of Shillington there is another moat. There appears to have been three Manor Houses here: Shillington, Shillington Bury and Apsley Bury.

The present day Shillington Manor was an 18th century House, which may have been built on an earlier site. Captain R. B. Lucas bought the House in 1911 but it was destroyed by fire during World War I. Lucas rebuilt it as a mock 18th century Manor House. That House was demolished in 1992 and replaced by a Georgian style House. The House remains in private hands.

Shillington, anciently Sethlingdone, in the Hundred of Clifton and Deanery of Shefford, lies about four miles from that town. Until the Dissolution of the Monasteries (1536-41), Ramsey Abbey (Huntingdonshire) held the Manor. At its dissolution, in 1537, it formed part of the Royal Honour of Ampthill, conferred on Princess Elizabeth and remained in Crown hands until after James I.

The Abbey leased Shillington Manor, in 1476, to Thomas Rotherham, Archbishop of York, who left it at his death, in 1500, to his nephew, Thomas Rotherham. His grandson Thomas and his wife Alice were later heirs, followed by George, their son, who held the Manor from 1561 to 1599, presumably leased from the Crown. Then came his son John who transferred this Manor to Sir Robert Napier, it remaining in the Napier family until the death of Sir John Napier, the last Baronet, in 1714. In 1748 Sir Conyers D'Arcy, held the Manorial Court and in 1759 Robert Darcy, 4th Earl of Holderness held the Court. In 1760 the Earl sold the Manor to Joseph Musgrave and, as Apsley Bury, it remained in the Musgrave family until at least 1908.

John Briscoe left Shillington Bury, in 1764, to Henry, Earl of Sussex, for life, which has caused Shillington Bury to be described, in some books and maps, as a Seat of the Earls of Sussex. After the Earl's death, Mr. Briscoe gave the Estate in fee to the heirs at law of the two daughters of Grey Longueville of Shillington. On the Earl's death, in 1800, one portion descended to Grey Arnold, whose father, Thomas Arnold, although a humble toll-gatherer at a turnpike near Dunstaple, and supporting a large family with a pittance, honourably refused to deprive his son of his patrimony, by selling his reversionary interest in this Estate, though the money arising from the sale would have rescued himself and family from poverty. This Thomas Arnold was a grandson of Margaret, the elder daughter of Grey Longueville. The other portion descended to the wife of George Antt, as representative of the younger daughter of Mr Longueville. We know little of the mid-19th century except for a sale by a Miss Profit to the father of William Hanscombe, Lord of the Manor in 1908.

The Manor of Aspley Bury, in this parish (but extending into Ion and Gravenhurst), is recorded as being occupied by Laurence Eton in 1556. By 1612, the Manor had passed through Richard Franklin to his son Sir John Franklin. John's sister Elizabeth married Sir Christopher Musgrave, and received Aspley Bury as her dowry. The Manor was held in 1757 by their son Joseph, whose nephew George held the property until he died in 1861. George Musgrave, his son, inherited and was succeeded by his son Edgar Musgrave, whose son Horace Edgar Musgrave owned the property in 1908, as well as Shillington Manor.

5 BATTLESDEN PARK

Battlesden House c.1818

Battlesden is a village about three miles from Woburn. In the 13th and 14th centuries, the family of Fermbaud, who twice represented the County in Parliament in the reign of Edward III (1327-77), held the Manor. In 1334 the King licensed Thomas Fermbaud to Impark 100 hectares of land and wood in Battlesden and Potsgrave. The Manor was afterwards possessed by the Chetwodes. About the reign of Queen Elizabeth I (1558-1603) it became the property of the Duncombes, by the marriage of William

Duncombe to Ellen, daughter and heir of William Saunders of Potsgrave.

It was one of this family, Sir Saunders Duncombe, a gentleman pensioner to James I and Charles I, who introduced sedan chairs in 1634; when he bought a patent which vested in him and his heirs the sole right of carrying persons "up and down in them," for fourteen years. It is probable that Sir Saunders, who was a great traveller, had seen them at Sedan in France, where they were first used.

In 1706 Allen Bathurst purchased the Manor of Battlesden and supposedly had the Manor House built, possibly on the site of an earlier House. A distinguished politician during the reigns of Queen Anne (1702-14) and George I (1714-27); he was created Baron Bathurst of Battlesden, in 1711. Battlesden continued for some years to be his country Seat, and the occasional resort of the celebrated constellation of wits, of whom he was the patron and friend. In 1724, Lord Bathurst sold Battlesden to Sir Gregory Page, Bart, of Blackheath, in Kent, whose daughter and heiress married Sir Edward Turner, Bart, of Ambrosden, in Oxfordshire, who died in 1736, leaving Sir Edward Turner, Bart, his heir. He also inherited the fortune of his uncle, John Turner, of Sunbury in Middlesex. Sir Edward married Cassandra, eldest daughter of William Leigh, of Adlestrop in Gloucestershire, and died at his home at Ambrosden in 1766. His eldest son, Sir Gregory Turner, Bart, succeeded him. In August 1795 he inherited the estates of his great uncle and godfather, Sir Gregory Page, Bart, and added the name and arms of Page, to his own. At the general election in 1784, he became MP for Thirsk, in Yorkshire, which he continued to represent in successive Parliaments until his death in 1805. Sir Gregory Osborne Page-Turner inherited his title and estates.

The Manor House was demolished in 1860 and replaced with a new 40-room House in 1864. Sir Joseph Paxton created the surrounding parkland and lake. However, Sir Edward Page-Turner, the owner, disliked the House and let it out before selling the Estate to Francis Russell, 9th Duke of Bedford in 1885. The Duke, already the owner of two Manor Houses in Bedfordshire, just wanted the land, so he ordered the House to be partially demolished in 1886. The ground floor was retained, which was used as a nursing home during World War I, then a maternity home in World War II. This was demolished after the War, leaving just the Garden House, which is a private dwelling today. Access to the Estate is provided by two identical lodges built in a style to match the House, one on the A5 Watling Street and the other on the A4012 near Milton Bryan. Both remain in existence although privately owned.

6 BILLINGTON MANOR

The Manor House in 2005

Arthur Macnamara of Caddington Hall (see Chapter 10) built the Manor House between the late 1870s and the early 1880s. He had Latin mottos: *Odi communi hominum*, engraved over each gable of the front entrance, which translates as: 'I hate common people'. The new House may have been erected on the site of the medieval Manor as one arm of an L-shaped moat was filled in when the House was built. Following Arthur Macnamara's death in 1906, his wife, Lady Sophia, remained in residence for three years. In 1909, Lady Sophia leased the House to Captain Gilliat, who bought it the following year. Hugh Bulkeley Price Brock occupied the property in 1914, and in 1920 Sir Richard Ashmole Cooper, Bart, MP lived there. Major Leigh Pemberton Stedall appears to have owned the House and lived there from about 1935 until his death in 1958. The House is a private residence today.

7 BLETSOE CASTLE

Bletsoe Castle c.1830

Bletsoe is a small village in the Hundred of Willey, and Deanery of Clopham, about six miles northwest of Bedford, on the road to Higham Ferrers. The Manor, at the time of the Domesday Survey (1086), was part of the large possessions of Hugh de Beauchamp; it was afterwards in the family of Pateshull. Mabel Pateshull, Lady of this Manor, founded the monastery of Grey Friars at Bedford, in the reign of Edward I (1272-1307). In 1327, John de Pateshull obtained the King's licence for embattling his

Mansion at Bletsoe. In 1344 he was summoned to parliament as a Baron. Sir Roger de Beauchamp, chamberlain to Edward III (1327-77), having married his eldest daughter, on a partition of the estates after the death of a son who died without issue, became possessed of this Manor, made it his chief seat, and was summoned to parliament in 1373 as Baron Beauchamp of Bletsoe. Margaret his granddaughter, became his heir on failure of the male line and married Sir Oliver St. John, a descendant of the ancient family of St. John of Basing, who already possessed large estates in the County, inherited from the Pavelys via the female line. She had one daughter, Margaret, by John Beaufort, Duke of Somerset, her second husband who married Edmund Tudor, Earl of Richmond, to become the mother of Henry VII (1485-1509). This illustrious lady, who was the founder of St. John's and Christ's Colleges in Cambridge, is said to have been born at Bletsoe. That her mother, the Duchess of Somerset, lived there in great state may be gleaned from the epitaph of Ralph Lannoy, formerly in Bletsoe church. He died in 1458, and is styled Cofferer (treasurer) and Keeper of the Wardrobe to Margaret, Duchess of Somerset, wife of Leo Lord Welles, her third husband. Sir Oliver St. John's like-named descendant was, in 1559, created Lord St. John of Bletsoe. Oliver, the 4th Baron, was, in 1624, advanced to the title of Earl of Bolingbroke. The Earldom became extinct in 1711. The Barony devolved to the posterity of Sir Rowland St. John, a younger son of Oliver Lord St. John, the 3rd Baron; and thence to his immediate descendant, Henry Beauchamp, Lord St. John, to whom the Manor of Bletsoe belonged. The Mansion, a large quadrangular building of typical early 17th century architecture, was pulled down long ago. The remains, equating to one side of the quadrangle, were converted into a farmhouse. Vestiges of the ancient castellated Mansion are visible near the farmhouse.

8 BROMHAM HALL

Rear of Bromham Hall c.1890

Bromham, in the Hundred of Willey and Deanery of Clopham, is a small village situated on the banks of the River Ouse about three miles from Bedford, near the road to Newport Pagnell. The Manor was, at the time of the Domesday Survey (1086), part of the large property of Hugh de Beauchamp, and upon the extinction of the male line of his family, became divided up and passed through the families of Munchensi, Tyes, Moubray, Boteler, Wake, Latimer, and Nevil. The Manor appears to have been united again in the 16th century. Sir John Dyve inherited it by female descent from the family of Wylde. Sir John died in 1607 and the Manor passed to his son, Sir Lewis Dyve, who became a distinguished Royalist officer during the Civil War (1642-51). Sir Thomas Trevor purchased it from the Dyves about the year 1707. He was created Baron Trevor of Bromham in 1711. The Manor House, although small and inconvenient, and from its situation near the River, liable to frequent floods, was for many years a country Seat of the Trevor family into the 19th century. The House has since been owned by the Rices and Wingfields, while Richard Skinner owned and occupied the property in 1927. It remains a private residence.

9 BUSHMEAD PRIORY

Bushmead Priory c.1730

Hugh de Beauchamp founded The Priory Church of Saint Mary, Bushmead, or Bushmead Priory, in Staploe parish for Augustinian Canons, in 1185. The community appears to have comprised the prior and up to four canons. The Priory prospered until the Dissolution (1536-41) when it was valued at £71 annual revenue. The site was granted, in 1537, to Sir William Gascoigne, Comptroller of the Household to Cardinal Wolsey. In

1545, Sir John Gascoigne sold it to Anthony Cocket, from whom, in 1552 it passed to William Gery of Over, in Cambridgeshire, and continued to be the residence of his descendants in the male line. Around 1735 Richard Gery took down the front building in the picture and erected a modern Mansion in its place (this itself was demolished in 1965). The building to the left of the picture, the refectory, survives and is now in the care of English Heritage and open to the public.

10 CADDINGTON HALL

Caddington Hall c.1910

Caddington Hall was a country Estate in Markyate parish. In the Domesday Book (1086), Caddington Manor was assessed at ten hides and was owned by Saint Paul's London. William Beckford of Fonthill, Wiltshire owned Caddington Manor in the late 18th century. John Pedley, who had political and commercial connections with Beckford, owned Zouches Farm in the west of the parish until by act of Parliament in 1804 he exchanged the farm for the Estate of Caddington Manor. There was a small House on the Estate that John Pedley had demolished and built Caddington Hall, which was completed around 1830. In 1835, John Pedley died, and Arthur Macnamara bought the Estate. The Macnamaras landscaped the grounds surrounding the House. In 1876, Caddington Hall passed to Arthur and Anne Macnamara's son, also called Arthur, who became squire of Billington and built the Manor House there. After his marriage in 1854 to Lady Sophia Eliza Hare, daughter of the 2nd Earl of Listowel, MP for St. Albans, the couple lived at Caddington Hall. Arthur Macnamara sold Caddington Hall about 1902 to Arthur Collings Wells. The House was demolished in 1975 to make way for urban development.

11 CHICKSANDS PRIORY

Chicksands Priory c.1829

About the year 1150, Pain de Beauchamp and Roese his wife, relict of Jeffery de Mandeville, founder of Walden Abbey, established a Priory at Chicksands for 120 nuns and 55 canons of the Order of St. Gilbert of Sempringham. The Priory was dissolved in 1538 and in the following year a grant was made of its site to Richard Snow. In 1576 it was purchased by Sir John Osborne, whose descendents held it until 1935. This family held important trusts for centuries under different British monarchs. During the Civil War (1642-51), the Osbornes were distinguished Royalists, and some family blood was spilt in the cause of Charles I (1625-49).

The House was originally the south canons' cloister, the north cloister being attached to the church, and is in the Hundred of Clifton, about a mile from Shefford. It remains extra parochial, although it exhibits much of a monastic appearance. About the middle of the 18th century, Sir Danvers Osborne had the House modernised by architect Isaac Ware (1704-66), removing the medieval features from the south and east fronts. Further restorations were made in Gothic Revival style by James Wyatt (1746-1813). In 1935, the Government bought Chicksands from the Osbornes. The Estate was developed for military purposes, and a large area of parkland was built over. The land remains in Ministry of Defence ownership, while the House has been restored for residential occupation.

12 COLMWORTH MANOR

Manor Farmhouse, Colmworth, 2015 cc-by-sa/2.0 **copyright** Bikeboy –
geograph.org.uk/p/4512136

Colmworth is a village in the Hundred of Barford and Deanery of
Eaton, about eight miles northeast of Bedford. The original, possibly
fortified, Manor House was early medieval with a moat, parts of which
remain around Manor Farmhouse (labeled Manor House on many

Ordnance Survey maps). Hugh de Beauchamp owned the Manor at Domesday (1086) and it continued in the Beauchamp line until it was sold to William Tooke in 1565. The Manor was transferred to Sir James Dyer, Lord Chief Justice of the Court of Common Pleas, in 1567. Lady Catherine Dyer had the present House built on the site of the medieval Manor House in 1609. Lodowick Dyer sold the Bedfordshire Estates to Richard Hillersdon around 1667 and the Manor stayed in the Hillersdon family until 1741 when it passed to the Ray family. Reverend Leonard Towne bought the Manor in 1797. He died in 1827 and the Manor passed to his daughter, Sarah Norris. Her family held the Manor into the 20th century.

The Colmworth Estate was sold by auction in 1918, Manor Farm being Lot 1 consisting of the six-bedroom House and 170 acres of land. The farm was bought by Harry Jordan, who had been the occupier for many years. During World War II the farm was used as an Air Raid Precautions post and the owner was Malcolm Arthur Aeneas Mackintosh. The owner in 1948 was Miss A. E. Church. Manor Farm, as the House is now called, is a private residence.

13 COLWORTH HOUSE

Colworth House 2002

Colworth, a hamlet of Sharnbrook as described in 1278, included Colworth Manor held by the Bedford Barony of Beauchamp. In 1278 William Fruel held it and in 1417 it was held by Baldwin Pigot, who was overlord by descent. The earliest tenant was John Druel who held half a hide in Colworth in 1278–9. In 1304 he obtained recognition of his right to the Manor from William Warren. John Druel's son, John, passed Colworth Manor to his brother Giles in 1331. Within the following generation

Colworth passed to Sir Thomas Greene who died in 1391-2 leaving sons Thomas and Henry. The Manor appears to have passed to Henry Greene, the younger son, for around 1415 Henry Greene's son John, relinquished his claims on the property to his brother Ralph. The following year, Sir Ralph Greene and his wife Katharine placed this Manor in trustee's hands. Ralph Greene died in 1417, when his brother John was declared to be his heir. The Manor passed (probably forfeited) to the Crown during the Wars of the Roses (1455-85). In 1484, Richard III (1483-5) granted Colworth to Thomas Lynom and his heirs for his good services against the rebels. Thomas Lynom either died without issue, or more likely, forfeiture by Henry VII (1485-1509), who had defeated Richard III at Bosworth, brought this Manor again into Crown possession.

The Crown granted the Manor to Sir Edward Montagu, in 1546/7. The Manor passed to his son, Sir Edward Montagu in 1557. Since there was an E-shaped Elizabethan House before the present House, this must have been built by him, possibly on the site of an earlier House. Sir Edward's son, Edward Montagu inherited the Manor in 1602. John Wagstaff bought the Manor in 1691 and sold it in 1715 to Mark Antonie. The present Colworth House was started almost immediately by Mark Antonie. Mark's son, John Antonie, chief clerk of the Court of King's Bench, inherited the Estate and built the main part of the House. John Antonie died in 1760 and the House passed to his brother Richard. On his death, in 1771, Richard Antonie bequeathed the Estate to a cousin, William Lee, (whose father of the same name, had been Lord Chief Justice of the King's Bench). William's son, also William, who had been obliged by Richard Antonie's will to add Antonie to his surname, inherited the Estate in 1778, later becoming an MP. William Lee-Antonie died in 1815 leaving the Estate to his nephew, the astronomer and antiquarian John Fiott, who adopted the surname of Lee. John Lee leased the House to Hollingworth Magniac in 1826 and sold him the Estate in 1854. Charles Magniac inherited it from his father in 1867 and sold it in 1891 to William Clarence Watson who modernised the House. Sir Albert Edward Bowen bought Colworth around 1912 and sold it around 1930 to Edgar Clayson, who sold it in 1935 to Henry Mond, 2nd Baron Melchett. Unilever bought the House in 1947 and developed the property into a research facility during 1948-1950, which employed around 1,750 people by the 1970s. In 2004 Unilever partnered with Arlington Securities to manage Colworth Science Park, aiming to attract science businesses, academics and entrepreneurs. Arlington was later acquired by Goodman, a property group. Since 2015, Palmer Capital and Wrenbridge Land have taken over management of the Science Park. Colworth remains one of Unilever's six research centres at home and abroad, employing around 750 staff.

A Channel 4 *Time Team* investigation of Colworth House grounds, following numerous finds by local amateur archaeologists, led to the discovery of a Roman villa and farm in an adjacent field. That particular programme was first broadcast on 22 February 2009.

14 GOLDINGTON BURY

The site of Goldington Bury. Map Data: copyright 2019 The GeoInformation Group, Google

Goldington Bury appears towards the end of the 14th century in the Pycard family. William Pycard was killed by his wife Joan. She was pardoned and in 1381 transferred Goldington Manor to Thomas Haselden. The Haselden family continued to hold this Manor until the early 18th century, when they appear to have sold it, around 1742, to the Becher family after the death of Robert Haselden. The House was rebuilt in the

18th century. In 1765 Goldington Bury was owned by Mr Addington. Silvester Addington, presumably the son, owned the Manor in 1797 and died in 1811. The Estate was auctioned in 1818 by William Addington and bought by Robert Elliott who died in 1844 leaving the Estate to his widow and their son Robert. In 1853, Robert died shortly followed by his widow, leaving their two daughters to inherit under the guardianship of their aunt, Elizabeth who was married to William Kenworthy Browne. The House was leased out for some years until the Estate was again auctioned in 1875 and bought by J. Shuttleworth, who died in 1883, passing the Manor to his son Colonel Frank Shuttleworth. The Shuttleworth family owned Goldington Bury until 1950, when it was up for sale by auction by the trustees of the Richard Ormonde Shuttleworth Remembrance Trust. Bedford Borough Council acquired the property in 1953, eventually demolishing the House around 1964. A tower block now covers the House platform and part of the old grounds are used by Bedfordshire County Cricket Club. The entrance lodge remains.

15 HARROLD HALL

Harrold Hall and Church c.1830

Harrold, a small market town on the River Ouse, bordering
Northamptonshire, lies in the Hundred of Willey, and Deanery of
Clopham, about nine miles from Bedford. Sampson le Fort founded a
Priory at Harrold, in honour of St. Peter, in 1150. Originally it was for
canons and nuns of the order of St. Nicholas of Arrouasia, but it later
housed a prioress and a few nuns of the order of St. Austin. The Knights
Templars and the family of Pabenham, appear to have been the principal

landowners in this parish, in the 13th and early 14th centuries. After the Dissolution (1536-41) the site was leased, in 1544, to William Lord Parr, and again, in 1555, to John Cheney and William Duncombe. London grocer, Ralph Farrar, bought the land and Priory buildings in 1558 when the lease expired. Ralph died in 1560 and his property was divided between his two sons, Francis, the eldest, getting the Priory, upon the site of which he built Harrold Hall between 1608 and 1610. Francis Farrer died in 1616 and the House passed to Sir Thomas Boteler, his son-in-law, who leased out the Hall. Sir Oliver Boteler became the tenant in 1653. In 1702 the Botelers, sold Harrold Hall to Anne Joliffe, who died in 1732. Her property passed to Anne Alston, her niece, who married Richard Mead, the famous physician. She died in 1762 and her Estate passed to Sir Thomas Alston of Odell, her nephew. The Alstons mainly leased out Harrold Hall, although the owner lived there in 1816 and extended the House. Rowland Crewe Alston sold Harrold Hall to Arthur Cecil Tyrrell Beck, in 1907, only to buy it back in 1912. In 1934 the Alston family put Harrold Hall Estate up for auction but it apparently did not find a buyer. It was conveyed to Edgar Clayson in 1938 and was taken over by the Pioneer Corps during World War II. Harrold Hall went to auction again in 1949 and became a private residence until 1961, when it was demolished to make way for urban development. Hall Close now occupies the site.

16 HAZELLS OR HASELLS HALL

Aerial view of the Hall. Map Data: copyright 2018 Infoterra Ltd & Bluesky, Google

Hasells Manor, in Sandy, was a Grange of the Priory of Chicksands, dating back to at least the 13th century. After the Dissolution (1536-41) Henry VIII (1509-47) granted Hasells Manor, in 1542, to Francis Pygott, who almost immediately transferred it to Robert Burgoyne. John Burgoyne sold the Manor in 1633, to Ephraim Huit, who sold it to Robert Brittain the following year. It remained in the Brittain family until 1721 when Baron Britain sold the Manor to Heylock Kingsley who rebuilt the Hall. He died in 1749 leaving the Manor to his daughter who had married William Pym of Radwell in 1748. The Manor remained in the Pym family into the 20th century. The House, service wing, cottages, outbuildings, and stables were restored and converted into 12 self-contained houses, cottages, apartments and flats around 1980.

17 HAWNES OR HAYNES PARK

Haynes Park 2001. Photo By Stephen Richards, CC BY-SA 2.0,
https://commons.wikimedia.org/w/index.php?curid=34065284

The Park, first recorded in 1312 as the Manor of Hawnes of around 240 acres (100ha). The present Haynes Park Mansion is Grade I listed and was built in 1720 for John (Lord) Carteret, 2nd Earl Granville, Lord President of the Council, 1751-63. It was remodelled in 1790 and is constructed to a square plan of red and white brick in two storeys with slate roofs. John Thynne, 3rd Baron Carteret inherited the Estate, which then extended to 800 acres (320ha). The Baron died without issue, and the the property passed to Lord John Thynne, sub-Dean of Westminster, his nephew. Francis John Thynne, his son, inherited the Estate on his father's death in

1881. In 1908 Mr. W. B. Greenfield lived at Haynes Park. In 1929 the House became Hawnes Girls School, a boarding school which closed in 1975 and was taken over by Clarendon School after their premises in Wales had burnt down. In 1992 Clarendon School closed and sold the property to an Indian spiritual organisation which relishes under the title of Radha Soami Satsang Beas British Isles (RSSB). Science of the Soul, their associated body, still occupies Haynes Park.

18 HOCKCLIFFE GRANGE

Aerial view of the Grange. Map Data: copyright 2018 Google

The present House dates from the 17th century but from its proximity to the church and earthworks, appears to be a replacement for an earlier dwelling. In 1616 Robert Gilpin was Rector of Hockliffe and the Estate was bought for him by his family. On Robert's death, the Grange seems to have passed to his son Richard. Thomas Gilpin (1704-1763) remodelled and extended the House in the Georgian Style and Richard Thomas Gilpin made significant alterations in the 19th century. Colonel Richard Thomas Gilpin died in 1882 and ownership passed to Peter Valentine Purcell through his marriage to Amy Gilpin. He lived in Kilcullen, County Kildare and let the property out until 1917 when the Hockliffe Grange Estate, with 54 acres of land, was put up for auction. Having failed to achieve its reserve price the Grange was not sold until 1923, when it was bought by Thomas Neville, a partner in the building firm of T & E Neville of Luton. Today the Grange remains a private residence.

19 HOUGHTON PARK HOUSE

Houghton Park House c.1770

The Old House at Houghton is now a picturesque ruin, it was built by Mary, daughter of Sir Henry Sydney, wife of the 2nd Earl of Pembroke, and was granted, at the Restoration (1660), to Robert Lord Bruce, who was created Viscount Bruceof Ampthill, and Earl of Aylesbury, in 1664; he was also made High Steward of the Honour of Ampthill.

The Bruce family were resident at Houghton Park House until 1696 when Thomas Bruce, 2nd Earl of Aylesbury, 3rd Earl of Elgin went into exile because of his loyalty to the deposed James II of England and Ireland, VII of Scotland (1685-8).

Thomas Bruce did not return and in 1738 John Russell, 4th Duke of Bedford, bought the House. The Duke's main residence was Woburn Abbey, some seven miles away. His son, Francis Russell, Marquess of Tavistock, took up residence at the House from 1764 until his death in a hunting accident in 1767. His grandson, Francis Russell, 5th Duke of Bedford, inherited the 4th Duke's titles and estates, which included Houghton Park. The 5th Duke attempted to let the House but having previously let the deer park; he could not secure a tenant for the House with no grounds. In 1794 he ordered Houghton Park House to be dismantled to reduce his liabilities. The Duke never married and died in 1802 without a male heir.

English Heritage now owns the ruins which can be visited free during daylight hours.

20 HOWBURY HALL

Aerial view of the Hall. Map Data: copyright 2019 Infoterra Ltd & Bluesky; Google

Howbury Hall is in Renhold parish three miles northeast of Bedford. In 1538 Sir John Nevill gave Renhold Manor to Sir John Gostwick, and it remained in the Gostwick family until 1624. Sir William Becher purchased the Howbury Estate from the Gostwick family about the year 1603 and the Becher family retained it until the male line died out. The Estate was then sold to Nathaniel Polhill in 1781 and has remained in the Polhill family. The old Hall, set in a park of about 100 acres (40ha), was almost destroyed by

55

fire in 1847, which burnt the west wing to the ground. Frederick Charles Polhill-Turner rebuilt the House, retaining the east wing, which was completed in 1852. Anthony Nathaniel Polhill inherited the House from his uncle in 1957. The property was found to be rotten and infested with death-watch beetles; the east wing was demolished the following year, and the House restored; remaining a private home to this day. An old amphitheatre is nearby.

21 HULCOTE HOUSE

Hulcote House c.1775

Holcot or Hulcote Manor had been granted to William Speke at the 1086 Domesday Survey. Overlordship later passed to the Beauchamp family of the Barony of Eaton. It is last mentioned in 1428. In 1086, Ralph Passwater was the Manor's tenant. His descendant Gilbert Passwater was Lord of the Manor in the 13th century. In 1337 William Passwater conveyed the Manor to Nicholas Fermbaud. In 1366 Katherine Fermbaud held the Manor with her husband John Woodville. Thomas Fermbaud alias Woodville held the Manor in 1428. In 1449 the Lord of the Manor was Sir Richard Woodville. Margaret Helwell, a descendant, married Thomas Sherard, and produced two sons, Richard and George. In 1541 George Sherard transferred the Manor to his brother Richard, who sold it later that year to Robert Chernock.

The Chernock family remained Lords of the Manor until Sir Villiers Chernock died in 1779. The Manor then passed to his nephew Edward Hervey who left no male heirs, his estates passing to his sister Elizabeth Chauncey, who divided them between her great-nieces. Part of the Manor went to William Montague. George Henry Montague held half the Manor in 1826. His heir was a Mr Bennett who held half of the Manor into the 20th century. The other half of the Manor went to Charlotte Orlebar Smith, and was divided between Charles Villiers Downes, her great-grandson and her grandson Boteler Chernock Smith.

The House survived at least until 1812 but was much dilapidated by then. Aerial and satellite photographs show earthworks northeast of the church, indicating the site of the medieval Manor House, its garden and fishponds. The House was rebuilt in 1575, and the ponds were probably incorporated into the landscaped garden at some point.

22 ICKWELL BURY

Ickwell Bury 2013. Photo copyright Bikeboy -geograph.org.uk/p/3787972
(cc-by-sa/2.0)

John Harvey built Ickwell Bury, close to the site of an earlier Manor House, in 1683. The Harvey family owned the House until 1925.

In 1898, Kelly's Directory records the owner of Ickwell Bury as John

Edmund Audley Harvey and described the property as a Mansion of red brick, in the Queen Anne style. The House stood in parkland of some 500 acres (200ha) and was approached via a mile-long avenue of trees.

In 1900, John Cunningham Thomson rented the House to relocate his Horton Preparatory School from Northamptonshire. Thomson sold the school in 1920 to Reverend George Lindsay Deuchar. The Harveys auctioned Ickwell Bury in 1924 but it failed to sell and then Deuchar's wife purchased it from the family by private treaty. Over the next few years, the school struggled to make a profit, and it merged with a similar school from Heddon Court in Cockfosters, Herts in 1933. The merger improved the situation for a few years, but in 1937 the school closed and most of the empty House was destroyed by fire shortly afterwards.

Colonel George Hayward Wells, who was chairman of Charles Wells brewery, bought the property and built a new smaller replacement House. He willed the Ickwell Bury Estate to Bedford School. The school used the grounds for field studies and as a conservation reserve. For a number of years, the school let Ickwell Bury House to the Yoga Health Foundation.

Bedford School sold Ickwell Bury into private hands in 1999 and followed by selling its surrounding land and buildings in 2013-14.

23 LUTON HOO

Luton Hoo c.1820

The Domesday Book (1086) does not record Luton Hoo Manor, but the de Hoo family occupied a Manor House here for four centuries. The Manor passed to the Rotherham family (and later the Napier family) when Thomas Hoo, 1st Baron Hoo and Hastings died in 1455. In 1751 Miss Napier left the House to her relative, Francis Herne, MP for Bedford. Francis Herne sold the Estate in 1762 to John Stuart, 3rd Earl of Bute, who was Prime

Minister from 1762 to 1763. Bute remodelled an earlier House to the designs of the neoclassical architect Robert Adam. Construction began in 1767 and seven years later the (incomplete) House was inhabited. At the same time Capability Brown redesigned the Park, which was enlarged from about 300 acres (120 ha) to 1,200 acres (490 ha). Brown dammed the River Lea to form two lakes, one of which extends to 60 acres (24 ha).

In about 1830 John Crichton-Stuart, 2nd Marquess of Bute, grandson of the 3rd Earl, transformed the House to the designs of Robert Smirke (1780-1867), the leading architect. Smirke redesigned the House (except for the south front) to resemble its present form today, complete with a massive portico, similar to that designed by Adam but never built. In 1843, a devastating fire destroyed much of the House and its contents.

In 1848, Liverpool solicitor and property speculator, John Shaw Leigh, purchased the Estate with burnt-out House. He married Hannah Blundell-Hollinshead, daughter of the Mayor of Liverpool (1791-4 & 1807) Henry Blundell (1755-1832), who owned Orrell, Blackrod and Pemberton collieries near Liverpool. Leigh rebuilt the derelict shell to Smirke's design. In 1871, his son John Gerard Leigh (1821-1875), inherited the Estate and married Eleanor Louisa Hawkes the following year. Eleanor was widow of Hon. Humble Dudley Ward (1821-1870) and daughter of Thomas Hawkes. John Gerard Leigh died childless in 1875, only three years after his marriage. He left all his money to his wife Eleanor, together with a life-interest in Luton Hoo, with remainder to his nephew Henry Leigh. In 1883, Eleanor married Christian Frederick de Falbe (1828-1896), the Danish Ambassador to the UK, becoming known as "Madame de Falbe". She was also a close friend of the Prince of Wales and entertained lavishly. In 1899 Madame de Falbe died, and the Estate returned to her first husband's nephew, Captain Henry Gerard Leigh (1856-1900), 1st Life Guards, married to Marion Lindsay Antrobus, daughter of Hugh Lindsay Antrobus. He died within a year of inheriting Luton Hoo, leaving an 11-year-old son John Cecil Gerard Leigh (1889-1963), on whose behalf Luton Hoo was sold.

In 1903, diamond magnate Sir Julius Wernher, who had been a tenant since 1899, bought the House. Wernher remodelled the interior to the designs of Arthur Davis and Charles Mewes, architects of the Ritz Hotel in

London. The roof was remodelled, to increase the amount of staff accommodation and casement windows were added.

The lavish redesign of the interior in the belle époque style resulted in a magnificent backdrop for Wernher's famous art collection. The marble-walled dining room displayed Beauvais tapestries while the massive Blue Hall at the centre of the House, displayed further tapestries, Louis XV furniture, and Sèvres porcelain.

The marriage of Harold Augustus Wernher, Julius's son, to Anastasia de Torby, a descendent of the former Russian Imperial family known as "Lady Zia" enhanced the magnificent art collection. She brought with her a stunning assemblage of Renaissance enamels and Russian artefacts, including works by Fabergé. For many years, the House and collection were open to the public. Many of the Fabergé items were stolen in the 1990s.

During World War II, the House served as Headquarters Eastern Command. Luton Hoo's Estate was used as a tank testing ground for Churchill tanks produced in Luton factories.

Following Lady Zia's death in 1977, her grandson Nicholas Harold Phillips inherited the Estate, but he died in 1991 and the House was again sold. The art collection is now on permanent display at Ranger's House in Greenwich, London.

The House has now been converted into a luxury hotel called the Luton Hoo Hotel, Golf, and Spa, which opened on 1 October 2007. It has 228 bedrooms and suites. The second floor of the House was rebuilt as part of the restoration project included in the plans drawn up by the original architects. Elite Hotels, the owners claim to have selected furnishings sympathetic to the House's former glory. The descendants of Sir Julius and Lady Alice Wernher have retained ownership of the surrounding Estate.

David Villanueva

24 MELCHBOURNE PARK

Melchbourne Park 2002. Photo copyright <u>Stephen Richards-</u>
<u>geograph.org.uk/p/3340963</u> - <u>cc-by-sa/2.0</u>

The Domesday Book (1086) records that Melchbourne was part of the estates of the Bishop of Coutance. Apparently, it reverted to the Crown following the Bishop's death. During the reign of Henry II (1154-1189), Alice, Countess of Pembroke founded the Preceptory of the Knights Hospitallers at Melchbourne and gave the Manor to them. Henry VIII (1509-47) dissolved the Preceptory and Edward VI (1547-53) gave the Manor to John, 1st Earl of Bedford. The Earls of Bedford held the Manor until Edward sold the Manor in 1608 to Oliver, Lord St. John of Bletsoe. About 1620 the 4th Baron St. John built a Mansion on the present site and moved there from Bletsoe Castle.

During the 18th century, the Mansion was remodelled; the present Georgian front, being created in 1741. The Parks and Lakes at the front of the House were probably laid out in the second half of the 18th century; a Deer Park being mentioned in 1766. Towards the end of the century, the Earldom died out and the Barony passed to relatives in Northamptonshire. In the 1780s the 12th Lord St. John moved to Melchbourne and further modernised the House.

The St. Johns owned the property until the 1930s and during World War II, the United States Air Corps occupied the House for a time. The Parks were mostly turned into arable land and have remained so.

After the War, Lawson Johnston refurbished the Mansion and lived there until he sold it to Peter Hempson in 1983. It has now been divided into around a dozen luxury flats.

25 MILTON-BRYEN

Milton-Bryen 1811

Milton-Bryant, (now Milton Bryan) and formerly Milton-Bryen, in Manshead Hundred, and Deanery of Dunstaple, is located two and half miles (4km) northwest of Toddington The Manor's history can be traced back to 1066 when it was held by Auti, a housecarl of Earl Aelfgar. After the Norman Conquest (1066) the Beauchamp family held the Manor as overlords. In 1266 John de Beauchamp died at the Battle of Evesham fighting against Henry III (1216-1272). John's three sisters then shared the Beauchamp lands with the overlordship of Milton Bryen Manor passing to Maud Beauchamp who married Roger de Moubray. After Roger de Moubray's death, Maud married Sir Robert Lestrange who died in 1312. Maud's grandson, John de Moubray was her heir. He joined Earl Thomas of Lancaster's rebellion against Edward II (1307-1327) and was captured at the Battle of Boroughbridge in 1321 and hanged at York as a traitor. Edward II gave his favourite, Hugh le Despenser, de Moubray's former Manors that same year. In 1326 Despenser was executed for treason and the Crown took all his estates. On Edward II's deposition in 1327 the overlordship returned to John de Moubray's son John. There is no mention of the overlordship after 1470.

Overlords frequently leased Manors out to tenants. William Froissart was a tenant of Milton Manor in 1086, as was the Bryen family, from the late 12th century. Their name was added to Milton to distinguish the Manor from Milton Ernest. In 1344 John Bryen transferred the Manor to Woburn Abbey.

When Woburn Abbey was dissolved, in 1538, the Crown took Milton Bryen Manor and, in 1542, attached it to the Honour of Ampthill. Elizabeth I (1558-1603) gave the Manor to Michael and Edward Stanhope in 1599 and in 1601 Christopher Estwick bought the Manor from Michael Stanhope. When Christopher died in 1611 his son, Christopher inherited the Manor. In 1626 Sir Francis Staunton bought the Manor. Around 1655 William Johnson bought the Manor from Staunton's grandson. The Johnson family probably built the current Manor House on the site of an earlier House, surrounded by a moat.

William Johnson left the Manor to his son Thomas, who was High-Sheriff of the County in 1702 and 1703. Following Thomas's death in 1707, his son Joseph inherited and was also High-Sheriff, in 1726 but died in 1742 without issue. He left the Manor to Henry Johnson, his third cousin. When Henry died in 1771 his daughter, Catherine inherited the Manor.

In 1784 Catherine married Sir Hugh Inglis who she predeceased in 1792 leaving the Manor to Sir Hugh. He was an East India Company director and in 1801 was made a Baronet. On his death in 1820, his son Robert inherited the Manor. Robert was an MP and was appointed High-Sheriff of Bedfordshire in 1824. He died childless in 1855, leaving the Manor to his widow, who left it to a Miss Thornton. In 1898, Miss Henrietta L. Synnot was Lady of the Manor which the Duke of Bedford bought from her in 1906. Miss Synnot continued to live there until 1924. Major Charles Edward Thornton was recorded as living there between 1928 and 1940.

The Manor House was listed in 1952 as Grade II, of special interest. At that time it was divided into two dwellings called The Manor House and Inglis House. The House is still residential today.

26 MOGGERHANGER HOUSE

Moggerhanger House 2010. Photo by John Brightley, CC BY-SA 2.0,
https://commons.wikimedia.org/w/index.php?curid=12549008

Moggerhanger was originally in Blunham Parish but after the church was built in 1860 it was separated to become Mogerhanger parish. Records show Roger de Trumpington holding the Manor until he died in 1289. The Manor descended to Roger's son, Giles, and was held by the Trumpingtons until 1457 when Eleanor, Sir Walter Trumpington's daughter, became engaged to Richard Enderby. Sir Walter gave the Manor to Richard's mother, Maud for life. In 1474, when Maud died, Richard took over the Manor until his death in 1487. John, his son, then sold the Manor to William Gascoigne.

By 1549 John Aleyn owned the Manor. In 1677 George Wyan transferred the Manor to three merchants, who kept it for a year then sold it to John Platt of Saint Giles in Middlesex. The Astells bought the Manor from John Platt after 1687.

Almonds farmhouse, later known as Morhanger or Muggerhanger Lodge, a red-brick villa, stood on the site of the current Mansion in the early 18th century. Richard Astell bequeathed the House, in 1777, to Robert Thornton, his nephew, who sold it to Godfrey, his brother. Godfrey became the Bank of England's Deputy Governor 1791-3 and Governor 1793-5. He hired the Bank's architect, John Soane (1753-1837) to renovate the House. Soane worked on the House from around 1790 until 1812, first for Godfrey and then for Stephen, Godfrey's son, who inherited the Estate in 1805. Humphry Repton (1752-1818) designed the gardens in the 1790s.

The Thornton family owned the Estate until 1864. The Dawkins from Over Norton, Oxon, were the next owners in 1857 and then Richard Mercer about 1888. The Fane family bought it from Colonel Algernon Mercer, his son, in 1909, and owned it until 1916.

Following some renovation, the House was used by a college until 1919 when the Bedfordshire County Council bought it and turned the building into a TB sanatorium. In 1957, its name was changed to Park Hospital and it specialized in orthopaedic cases until it closed in 1987. The former Hospital was disused until 1995, when Harvest Vision, an evangelical trust, bought it. The Moggerhanger House Preservation Trust was set up in 1997 to renovate the building and turn it into a conference and training centre, which opened to the public in 2005.

27 NEWBURY MANOR

Newbury Manor House 1812

The Domesday Book records Newbury Manor, Silsoe, was held by Nigel d'Aubigny in 1086. The d'Aubigny family continued to hold the Manor, but Ralph FitzRichard held it by 1284. The FitzRichards held the main part of the Manor for over a hundred years but transferred a quarter to Ralph de Limbury and others in 1302. By 1346 John Morice held this quarter of the Manor, through Margaret, his wife and by 1428 it had passed to John Wayte. Sometime later the quarter was reunited with the main part of the Manor.

In 1528 Henry Wayte sold the Manor to Edward Daniell and the Daniell family held it until 1686 when Robert Nicholls of Saint Albans bought the Manor from William Daniell. The House was built in the late 16th century, possibly replacing a moated house a little to the north-east.

In 1775 Robert's daughters sold the Manor of Newbury to the executors of the Duke of Kent bringing it into the ownership of Jemima, Marchioness Grey and thus merging it with the Manor of Wrest. (See Chapter 37) Newbury Manor House became a farmhouse for Newbury Farm, which was let out to various tenants.

In 1908, Samuel Paterson rented Newbury Farm from the 9th Baron Lucas of Crudwell, who owned the Wrest Park Estate. Samuel Paterson bought the farm in 1918 and still lived there in 1931.

In 1981, Newbury Farm was sold and remains in business today. The farmhouse is now called Newbury Manor.

28 OAKLEY HOUSE

The Mansion about 1820

Oakley House is situated upon the north bank of the River Ouse and appears to have been built between 1748 and 1750 as a hunting Lodge for the Duke of Bedford. An earlier Mansion House later called the Burystead was located to the southeast of the present House. The House and grounds were remodelled between 1787 and 1792 and described as follows: at the entrance to the Paddock is a Rustic Lodge; the walls and roof of which are nearly covered with roses and eglantine; the road winding amidst tall elms towards the House: on the left are convenient Stables, Coach Houses, and the Dog-Kennel. On the north of the House, the ancient carriage front, is now a very capacious Kitchen Garden, with Hot-Houses and Conservatories. The entrance is on the east, under a rustic colonnade, having four niches in the outer wall adorned with marble statues; from the House the path continues by a long arch of foliage round the garden, towards a sloping meadow, from where the above view of the south front of the Mansion was taken. The garden is divided from the meadow by a ha-ha fence; at the bottom of which flows the river, forming the southern boundary.

On this front of the House we see the full effect of the judicious alteration of the ancient building: a wide Terrace and Veranda running round the base contract the height and add extent and space; the bricks of which it is constructed now assume the appearance of stone: vases of various forms, containing flowers, are placed upon the Terrace.

The Garden is laid out in the French style and is neatly kept; its character is elegance and beauty. The lawn is diversified with beds or baskets of roses, which are also placed amid rockwork, and the paths wind in devious tracks round borders, with a colourful profusion of rare plants. In other parts it is more regular, and on a pedestal is a gilded sphere, forming the centre of a circular trellis covered with honeysuckle, jasmines, and several kinds of creeping plants: on the west are ash, chestnut, and other trees feathering down to the turf.

The Duke died in 1771 and the title and ownership passed to his grandson aged six years. Robert Hampden, Lord Trevor leased the House in 1772 for fourteen years. Successive Dukes owned the Mansion until 1918 when the Duke sold The Oakley Estate privately to his cousin the 2nd Baron Ampthill who lived there until his death in 1935, when Oakley House was sold again. Charles M. Wells was the occupier in 1936. The House has been sold a number of times since, most recently in 2008.

29 ODELL CASTLE

Odell Castle 1811

Before 1066 Levenot, a thegn of Edward the Confessor owned the land. Both the village and land were then called Wahull. William I (1066-1087) gave the Manor and title, Baron of Wahull, to Walter de Flandrensis. The Baron built a motte-and-bailey castle, with a stone keep, on the land. The family lived here for some 400 years.

In 1542, with no male heir the title died out and came into the possession of Agnes Woodhall, daughter of Anthony de Wahull, who later married Richard Chetwode. Upon her death in 1576 it passed to her son Richard Chetwode, who appears to have remodelled the castle into a new House. William Alston (1607-38) bought the Estate from Richard Chetwode in 1633. William's brother, Sir Thomas Alston (1609-78), inherited the Estate and was created 1st Baronet Alston. His son, Sir Rowland Alston (1652-97), 2nd Baronet, inherited and left the House to his widow, Lady Temperance Alston, who later married Sir John Wolstenholme. Around 1705, Lady Wolstenholme considerably altered the inside of the House and rebuilt the northeast and southeast fronts. On Lady Wolstenholme's death, in 1728, the House passed to Sir Rowland Alston 4th Baronet (1679-1759); then to Sir Thomas Alston 5th Baronet (1724-74), his son. His wife ran off with a horse dealer in 1752, but he had two sons by his housekeeper, Margaret Lee, who inherited the House for life. Margaret died in 1809 and the House passed to her and Sir Thomas's eldest son, Thomas Alston (c.1755-1823). The House passed to his son, Justinian Alston (1780-1848) then to his son, Crewe Alston (1828-1901). In 1864-65, Crewe Alston rebuilt and heightened the southwest range and added a two-storey bay window. In the 1880s, the Agricultural Depression bankrupted him but the Estate was preserved as his inheritance was entailed and could not be sold. The Estate passed to Rowland Crewe Alston (1852-1933), his son. In 1930 the House was in such poor condition that Rowland moved out to a nearby bungalow 'on health grounds'. The following year the House was burned down by a fire that appears to have originated in the boiler room.

Sir George Lawson-Johnston, 1st Baron Luke (1873-1943) bought the House in 1934. His son, Ian St. John Lawson-Johnston 2nd Baron Luke (1905-96) built a new Manor House on the site in 1962, using the old stones but there is little left of the original castle; only crop marks and earthworks. The House was sold again in 1998.

30 OLD WARDEN PARK

The Mansion House 2007. Photo by Giles Keen, CC BY-SA 2.0,
https://commons.wikimedia.org/w/index.php?curid=6755286

Sir John Saint John built an earlier Old Warden Park House, near Biggleswade, about 1610 after pulling down an older property. Sir Samuel Ongley, a London merchant, bought the Old Warden Estate in the late 17th century. In 1785 the Estate passed to Robert, 2nd Lord Ongley, who probably laid out the Park. The 3rd Lord Ongley created the celebrated Swiss Garden between 1824-32 but later ran into financial difficulties. In 1872 Joseph Shuttleworth (1819-83) of Clayton & Shuttleworth, the Lincoln engineering company bought him out and Old Warden Park afterwards became better known as the Shuttleworth Estate.

In 1875-8 Joseph Shuttleworth employed the eminent Victorian architect, Henry Clutton (1819-93) to replace the previous House with the House which stands today. Clutton's design, in Jacobean style, with its high chimneys and 100ft high clock tower have defined and distinguished the House for more than a hundred years.

Dorothy Shuttleworth (1879-1968) lived in the House for most of her life. During both World Wars, she used the House as a Red Cross convalescent home. In 1940, her son Richard Ormonde Shuttleworth (1909–1940), a passionate aviator, was killed in a flying accident. Dorothy Shuttleworth set up the Shuttleworth Trust in 1944 in memory of her son. In 1946, the House became an agricultural college and Bedford College Services now manages Shuttleworth College next to the House on behalf of the Shuttleworth Trust. The adjacent Swiss Garden is leased to Bedfordshire County Council.

The Shuttleworth Trust now manages the grade II listed House as a wedding and corporate event venue. It is open to the public on selected event dates.

31 PAVENHAM BURY

Pavenham Bury c.1910

The House was formerly known as Berrystead Manor House, and its earliest recorded owner was Edward Vaux, 4th Baron Vaux of Harrowden (1588-1661); who sold the Manor in 1647 to John Alston (c.1614-87). The Manor passed to his son, William Alston (1637-1708) and then to William Alston (1665-1713), his son. In due course the Manor descended to his son, William Alston (1710-36), who bequeathed his Estate to his wife Ann for life, it was to be sold after her death, and the proceeds divided between his two sisters, Mary Lord, and Frances Brandreth. Ann Alston died in 1741. In

1745 the Estate was sold to John Franklyn. On his death, in 1748, the Estate passed to his brother Joseph, who died in 1762 and whose widow, Joan Franklyn, died in 1767, having instructed trustees to sell. In 1768, the Estate was sold to Richard Sutton, who subsequently sold it to Thomas Clark in 1778. Francis Green bought the Manor around 1837 and died in 1840, leaving the Manor to Thomas Abbott Green, his nephew. Thomas Abbot Green spent several thousand pounds remodelling the House and gardens then sold the Estate in 1849 to Richard Harvey, of St. Day, Cornwall, who was forced to sell it again in 1851 when it was bought by Joseph Tucker (1800-77). Mary Tucker, his daughter, inherited the Estate and later married Reverend William Burton-Alexander. In 1904, the Estate passed to their only son, Joseph Tucker Burton Alexander, who began to mortgage it heavily. By 1909, there was £39,000 owing on various mortgages which forced the sale of the Estate. The house itself was sold in 1919 to Sir George Lawson-Johnston (1873-1943), 1st Baron Luke (who later bought Odell Castle (Chapter 29)). His son Ian St. John Lawson-Johnston (1905-96), 2nd Baron Luke, inherited the House and let it to Sir Percy Laurie around 1950.

The House was badly damaged by fire in 1960 and demolished the following year: some parts were salvaged and used to remodel the former stables and coach house into a new House, now called Pavenham Court. A housing estate occupies the site of the Manor House and part of the park.

32 STRATTON PARK

Stratton Park c.1910

The Domesday Book (1086) contains four references to Stratton hamlet. Lord of Biggleswade Manor, Ralph de Lisle, held a Manor, formerly owned by Archbishop Stigand, assessed at four hides. This Manor seems to have become absorbed into Biggleswade, and passed with it to the Bishop of Lincoln, who in 1284 held half a fee in Stratton as part of Biggleswade Manor. Countess Judith held three and a half virgates, which later became Stratton Manor and part of the Honour of Huntingdon. When it was divided between the coheirs of John Earl of Huntingdon, his youngest sister, Ada, inherited the overlordship of Stratton and, on her marriage with Henry Hastings it passed to the Earls of Pembroke.

No connection has been found between the under tenant, Fulk de Paris, in the Domesday Book, and William Rixband, who held Stratton in 1231. The Rixband family continued holding the Manor, and in 1322 Margaret Rixband gave William Latimer her Stratton Manor in exchange for service. The Latimer family held the Manor until Elizabeth Latimer gave Stratton as her dowry in her marriage to Robert de Willoughby who died in 1397. Before his death, Robert had leased the Manor for an annual rent of £10 to Richard Enderby and his wife, Alice, and they later acquired full possession. Their son, John Enderby held the Manor at his death in 1457. His widow, Maude, went on to marry Robert Bothe, and when she died in 1474 the Manor went to Richard Enderby, her son by her first marriage. Richard died in 1487, when his son John acquired the Manor. John died in 1509 leaving only a daughter, Eleanor, to inherit. She married Francis Pygott, who, took exception to their eldest son Michael's marriage, disinheriting him and settling the Manor on Lewis, his son, with remainder going to Lewis's younger brother John. In 1588, Lewis and John transferred the Manor to Sir Edmund Anderson, chief justice of the Queen's Bench. The Andersons of Eyworth continued to hold the Manor until the death of Edmund Anderson in 1639 when his only daughter inherited and married Sir John Cotton. The Cottons renovated the Elizabethan Mansion and sold it to the Barnett family in 1764. The Barnetts refaced the House in 1878 and undertook quite a number of improvements over the next few years.

The last Barnett owners were Captain Charles Fitzroy Barnett and his wife Lucy. Charles died in 1887 followed by their only remaining son, Clayton, in 1900. Lucy died in 1908 and the Stratton Park Estate was sold in 1910. Bedfordshire County Council purchased a large area of land for renting, while local farmers and market gardeners bought the rest. James Clouston, of Seamer House School leased the Mansion, and it became Parkfield School for boys.

By 1939, the school had closed; the Army used the Mansion as a base during World War II and the Mansion became derelict. It was demolished in 1960 and replaced with a small housing development. Two moats at the

west side of the former park suggest that there were earlier Mansions on
this site.

33 SOUTHILL PARK

Southill Park 1829

Southill Park lies about two miles north of Shefford. Its predecessor was Gastlings, Gastlynbury or Gastlyns Manor and the overlord in the early 13th century appears to have been Albreda, Walter Espec's younger sister, who married Geoffrey de Trailly. Until 1438, the Manor was part of the Honour of Trailly.

In 1667, Sir John Keeling or Kelyng bought the Manor from John

Thurgood. The Keelings held the Manor until about 1707 when it was sold to Sir George Byng, 1st Viscount Torrington (1663-1733), who built the current House in the 1720s, replacing an earlier dwelling some distance away. Pattee Byng, 2nd Viscount Torrington inherited the Manor. It passed to George Byng, 3rd Viscount Torrington, his brother, then to George Byng, 4th Viscount Torrington. Samuel Whitbread (1720–1796), the brewer, bought the Estate in 1795. In the same year, Henry Holland (1745-1806) was commissioned to remodel the House.

Southill Park remains the home of the Whitbread family and is private property, not open to the public.

34 SUTTON PARK

**Aerial view of the Mansion. Map Data: copyright 2019 Getmapping plc;
Google**

The principal holder in Sutton at the time of the Domesday Survey
(1086) was Countess Judith, who held six hides, which subsequently became
Sutton Manor. Her lands became part of the Honour of Huntingdon.
Judith's daughter, Maud married David of Scotland, who later became Earl
of Huntingdon, and the Earls of Huntingdon held the Manor until the
death of John le Scot, Earl of Huntingdon, without issue, in 1237. His
sisters, Margaret, Isabel, and Ada each received a share of the overlordship.

The overlordship of Sutton passed to Isabel, the second sister, wife of Robert Bruce. Robert Bruce the elder, their son, was overlord in 1284 but his son Robert Bruce the younger, forfeited his English lands and overlordship went to Edward III (1312-1377) who gave it to his third son John O'Gaunt, 1st Duke of Lancaster, (1340-99). The supposed site of his Manor House is a large earthen mound encircled by a ditch north of the present House. Local tradition has it that the village was formerly nearby.

In 1086 eight tenants held lands of Countess Judith with holdings ranging from between half a hide and two hides. We cannot tell which of these holdings formed Sutton Manor, but it is probable that various portions became combined under one person. About 1168 when Richard de Reincourt was Lord of Sutton his daughter and heiress married Robert Foliot. Their son Richard Foliot inherited the Manor and around 1198 Margery, his only child, married Wyschard Ledet, who held the Manor in 1216. Christina Ledet, his daughter married Henry de Braybrooke in 1222 and he had already inherited from his father free tenements in Sutton. Christina survived her husband and married Gerard de Furnival. At her death, which occurred prior to 1271, her two granddaughters became coheirs. Of these Alice, the wife of William le Latimer inherited Sutton Manor as part of her share in Christina's estate. Alice le Latimer, in 1315, transferred the Manor to John de Kinnardseye, who granted it back for her life and then to Nicholas le Latimer and heirs. If the line died out, then the Manor was vested in Thomas Earl of Lancaster and his heirs. Following the death of Alice le Latimer, Nicholas gained Sutton Manor in 1317. By 1327 William le Latimer, Alice's son owned the Manor. William, his son, held Sutton when he died in 1336, and the Manor passed to his son, also William, who was under age at the time of his father's death. He died in 1381 leaving only a daughter Elizabeth, wife of John Neville of Raby, who held this Manor in right of his wife at the time of his death in 1389. In 1392 the son of John O'Gaunt, Duke of Lancaster, Henry Earl of Derby, successfully claimed Sutton Manor by right of Alice le Latimer's settlement in 1315 and during the 15th century it was part of the Duchy of Lancaster, and was the subject of various temporary grants. In 1402 Henry Longdon received the site of the Manor of Sutton for his life, and similarly in 1427 Elizabeth, wife of Thomas Swinford, and daughter of William Beauchamp of Powick was granted this Manor for life. The Duchy of Lancaster, settled the Manor in 1544 on Thomas Burgoyne and his heirs forever and it remained in the Burgoyne family into the 20th century.

Sutton Park House was destroyed by a fire in 1825 and rebuilt in 1859. The army requisitioned and used the House and Park during World War II. The House became dilapidated and was bought, along with the Park, by the Mid Beds Golf Club in 1947. The House was refurbished and became the clubhouse of the renamed John O'Gaunt Golf Club.

35 TEMPSFORD HALL

Aerial view of the Mansion around 2000. Map Data: copyright 2019 Infoterra & Bluesky; Google

In 1769 Sir Gillies Payne, Lord of Tempsford, Drayton and Brays Manors built himself a new House at Tempsford called Tempsford Hall. The Payne family owned the Hall until 1824 when Colonel William Stuart bought it. A fire occurred in 1898, causing rebuilding of the House in 1904. Towards the end of World War I, German prisoners-of-war were allowed to camp in the stables while they were set to work as ploughmen in the general area. A distant relative left the House to Stuart family member,

Kathleen Wynne, in 1933. The Special Operations Executive used the House as an agent reception and a pre-flight preparation centre during World War II. Henry Hales acquired the House following the War and used it as a clinic until 1964 when Kier Group, the construction firm, bought it as their headquarters.

36 WOBURN ABBEY

Woburn Abbey 1819

Woburn Abbey was founded in 1145, by Hugh de Bolebec, a powerful Baron, for Monks of the Cistercian order, at the instigation of the Abbot of Fountains. In 1547, the monastery and revenues, were granted by Edward VI (1547-53) to John, Lord Russell, who was created Earl of Bedford in 1550, and it has remained in the possession of that family ever since.

Francis Russell, the 4th Earl (1587-1641) and John's grandson, occupied Woburn Abbey from the 1620s. Within about ten years, Francis had added a two-storey wing to the north side of the House, as well as a grotto. Both of these additions are still a part of the House today. The architects Henry Flitcroft (1697-1769) and later, Henry Holland (1745-1806) largely rebuilt the Abbey from 1744 for John Russell the 4th Duke (1710-71). Flitcroft designed the State Apartments in the West Wing as well as an impressive Grand staircase featuring a wrought-iron balustrade. Flitcroft was also commissioned to design the Stable blocks in the grounds, which are referred to as North Court and South Court. They were built around 1750, shortly after the completion of the House construction.

While Flitcroft was responsible for the north portion of the House, Holland modernized the Abbey and redesigned the South side of the building. He also designed the Chinese Dairy located in the gardens and a large indoor riding school.

Sir William Chambers (1723-96), another prominent architect, was employed by the 4th Duke. The Duke used him to make occasional alterations, and he also built the Chambers Bridge separating the New Pond from the Basin Pond. John Russell, the 6th Duke (1766-1839) employed architect Sir Jeffry Wyatville (1766-1840), in 1816, to design the Holland Conservatory for the Duke's large sculpture collection. Although the Abbey was visited by many dignitaries over the years, a royal visit by Queen Victoria and Prince Albert in 1841 made a huge impact on the House. Ever since her visit, the room has been titled Queen Victoria's Bedroom. World War I brought further changes to the Abbey. Mary, Herbrand Russell the 11th Duke's wife, became a nurse and administrator by turning the riding school at Woburn Abbey into a military hospital.

From 1941, Woburn Abbey was the headquarters of the secretive Political Warfare Executive (PWE) which had its London offices at the BBC's Bush House.

After World War II, half the Abbey had to be demolished following the discovery of dry rot. The demise of Hastings Russell, the 12th Duke, in 1953 exposed his son, Ian Russell, the 13th Duke, to heavy death duties, and the Abbey was a half-demolished, half-derelict House. He could have handed the family estates to the National Trust but kept ownership and opened the

Abbey to the public in 1955. It gained popularity as other features such as Woburn Safari Park were created in the grounds in 1970.

In 1975, the 13th Duke relocated to Monte Carlo. Robin, Marquess of Tavistock, his son, and his wife ran the Abbey in his father's absence. Robin became the 14th Duke when his father died in November 2002 in Santa Fe, New Mexico, United States. On the death of the 14th Duke, in June 2003, his son Andrew became the 15th Duke, and continued his father's task of running Woburn Abbey Estate. The building is Grade I listed.

37 WREST HOUSE

Wrest House c.1819

Wrest House built 1834 -39. Photo by Nigel Cox, CC BY-SA 2.0,
https://commons.wikimedia.org/w/index.php?curid=4548970

Wrest House, Silsoe, was for a long time the residence of the ancient and illustrious family of the Greys, who possessed the Manor from the time of Roger de Grey, who died owner of it in 1353. Edward IV (1461-83) made Edmund Grey Lord Treasurer in 1463 and Earl of Kent two years later. Henry, last Duke of Kent, of this family, dying in 1740 without male issue, this Mansion descended to his granddaughter Jemima, Marchioness Grey, and at her death in 1797, she was succeeded by her eldest daughter, Lady Amabella Hume Campbell, Baroness Lucas, of Crudwell, a title granted in 1663 to the daughters and coheirs of John Lord Lucas, whose only daughter Mary, married Anthony Grey, 11th Earl of Kent (1645-1702).

The last Duke of Kent was very partial to this House, and adorned the Gardens, with Obelisks, Pavilions, and other buildings, particularly a magnificent Banqueting House, where, he spent many convivial hours with some great statesmen who were his contemporaries. The Pleasure Grounds were at the same time much improved by Capability Brown (1716-83).

The present House was built in 1834–39, to designs by Thomas de Grey, 2nd Earl de Grey (1781-1859), and nephew of Amabella Hume, from whom he inherited Wrest. He was an amateur architect who was inspired by French Chateaux.

On his death, the seat passed to his daughter, Anne, Countess Cowper, who became 7th Baroness Lucas. On her death, in 1880, her son, Francis Thomas de Grey Cowper, became 8th Baron Lucas and inherited Wrest.

In 1905, Francis died and was succeeded by Auberon Thomas Herbert, 9th Baron Lucas and 5th Lord Dingwall, his nephew, who leased the House to US Ambassador Whitelaw Reid in the same year. The Ambassador died there in 1912. Nan Ino Cooper, Baroness Lucas of Crudwell and Lady Dingwall (1880-1958) ran Wrest Park as a military hospital during World War I, until a fire in 1916 resulted in the hospital closing. Auberon was killed on active duty in the Royal Flying Corps in 1916. Nan inherited the House and sold it the following year to businessman John George Murray of Thirsk.

In 1939, while retaining the parkland, Murray sold the Mansion and surrounding grounds to the Sun (Alliance) Insurance Company which, in anticipation of the War, wanted to move its headquarters out of London.

The Sun Insurance remained at Wrest until the War ended, moving back to London in early 1946. The company sold Wrest Park to the Ministry of Works (now Department of Environment) in 1949. The Ministry leased the buildings to the National Institute of Agricultural Engineering. Silsoe Institute as it became known carried out research into farming, food and environmental management. The Institute closed in 2006 and English Heritage took over the management of the House and gardens. The gardens and part of the House are open to the public. The original park is mainly given over to agricultural use.

38 BIBLIOGRAPHY AND SOURCES

Bedfordshire Archives and Records Service, http://bedsarchives.bedford.gov.uk

James Collett-White, Ed. *Inventories of Bedfordshire Country Houses 1714-1830* (Bedfordshire Hist Rec Soc, 1995)

England's Lost Country Houses, http://www.lostheritage.org.uk/

English Heritage, https://www.english-heritage.org.uk/

Thomas Fisher, *Collections Historical, Genealogical and Topographical for Bedfordshire,* (London, 1836)

Genmaps, http://freepages.rootsweb.com/~genmaps/genealogy/index.html

Daniel and Samuel Lysons, *Magna Britannia*, (London, 1806)

Nick Kingsley, *Landed Families of Britain and Ireland,* http://landedfamilies.blogspot.com

Mervyn Macartney, *English Houses and Gardens in the 17th and 18th Centuries,* (London, 1908).

Moggerhanger, Bedfordshire, https://moggerhanger.uk/

F O Morris, *A Series of Picturesque Views of Seats of the Noblemen and Gentlemen of Great Britain and Ireland,* (London, 1860).

National Trust, https://www.nationaltrust.org.uk

J P Neale, *Views of the Seats of Noblemen and Gentleman in England, Wales, Scotland and Ireland,* (London, 1825).

William Page, Ed. *Victoria History of the County of Bedford,* (London, 1912).

William R Shepherd, *Historical Atlas,* (New York, 1911)

http://www.shillington-history.org.uk/Pages/Villagehisory/Village%20history.htm   (accessed 06.10.18)

J S Storer, *Antiquarian and Topographical Cabinet,* (London, 1810)

http://www.truetreasurebooks.net, Reprint of Bedfordshire Map, (c.1840)

A Vision of Britain through Time, http://www.visionofbritain.org.uk/

http://www.waymarking.com/waymarks/WM8M34_Shillington_Manor_Apsley_End_Shillington_Bedfordshire_UK (accessed 06.10.18)

BOOKS IN PRINT FROM THE SAME AUTHOR

THE SUCCESSFUL TREASURE HUNTER'S SECRET MANUAL: Discovering Treasure Auras in the Digital Age, Soft Cover, 230mm x 150mm, (9 x 6 inches) 97 pages, (CSIP, 2016), ISBN 978 1540747815

(Also an E-Book under the title: THE SUCCESSFUL TREASURE HUNTER'S SECRET MANUAL: How to Use Modern Cameras to Locate Buried Metals, Gold, Silver, Coins, Caches…)

CLEANING COINS & ARTEFACTS: Conservation * Restoration * Presentation, Soft Cover, 210mm x 146mm, (8.25 x 5.75 inches) 110 pages, (Greenlight Publishing, 2008) ISBN 978 1 897738 337

(Also an E-Book under the title: THE SUCCESSFUL TREASURE HUNTER'S ESSENTIAL COIN AND RELIC MANAGER: How to Clean, Conserve, Display, Photograph, Repair, Restore, Replicate and Store Metal Detecting Finds)

PERMISSION IMPOSSIBLE: Metal Detecting Search Permission Made Easy, Soft Cover, 210mm x 146mm, (8.25 x 5.75 inches) 78 pages, (True Treasure Books, 2007) ISBN 978 0 9550325 3 0 (Also an E-Book)

SITE RESEARCH FOR DETECTORISTS, FIELDWALKERS & ARCHAEOLOGISTS, Soft Cover, 250mm x 190mm, (9.75 x 7.5 inches) 160 pages, (Greenlight Publishing, 2006) ISBN 1 897738 285

SUCCESSFUL DETECTING SITES: Locate 1000s of Superb Sites and

Make More Finds, Soft Cover, 250mm x 190mm, (9.75 x 7.5 inches) 238 pages, (Greenlight Publishing, 2007) ISBN 978 1 897738 306

THE SUCCESSFUL TREASURE HUNTER'S ESSENTIAL SITE RESEARCH MANUAL: How to Find Productive Metal Detecting Sites, (E-Book)

THE ESSENTIAL GUIDE TO OLD, ANTIQUE AND ANCIENT METAL SPOONS, Soft Cover, 210mm x 146mm, 88 pages, (True Treasure Books, 2008) ISBN 978 0 9550325 4 7 (Also an E-Book)

DOWSING FOR TREASURE: The New Successful Treasure Hunter's Essential Dowsing Manual, Soft Cover, 230mm x 150mm, (9 x 6 inches) 96 pages, (CSIP, 2016) ISBN 978-1518766060 (Also an E-Book)

MY ANCESTOR LEFT AN HEIRLOOM: Discovering Heirlooms and Ancestors Through the Metalwork They Left Behind, Soft Cover, 210mm x 146mm, (8.25 x 5.75 inches) 84 pages, (True Treasure Books, 2011) ISBN 978 0 9550325 6 1

(Also an E-Book under the title: MY ANCESTOR LEFT AN HEIRLOOM: Hunting Family History and Genealogy Treasure Through Metal Detecting Finds)

METAL DETECTING MADE EASY: A Guide for Beginners and Reference for All, Soft Cover, 210mm x 146mm, (8.25 x 5.75 inches) 128 pages, (True Treasure Books, 2014) ISBN 978 0 9550325 7 8 (Also an E-Book)

FAITHFUL ATTRACTION: How to Drive Your Metal Detector to Find Treasure (E-Book)

TOKENS & TRADERS OF KENT in the Seventeenth, Eighteenth & Nineteenth Centuries, Soft Cover, 215mm x 140mm, (8.5 x 5.5 inches) 112 pages, (True Treasure Books, 2015) ISBN 978 0 9550325 8 5 (Also an E-Book)

HOW TO FIND BRITAIN'S BURIED TREASURE HOARDS, Soft Cover, 295mm x 210mm, (11.75 x 8.25 inches) 150 pages, (Greenlight Publishing, 2017) ISBN 978 1 897738 627

METAL DETECTING BENEFITS FOR LANDOWNERS, (with Jacq le Breton), Soft Cover, 230mm x 150mm, (9 x 6 inches) 28 pages, (CSIP, 2016) ISBN 978-1537341118 (Put your contact details on the back cover and give to landowners when requesting permission)

TREASURE HUNTING for PROFIT: With and Without a Metal Detector, Soft Cover, 230mm x 150mm, (9 x 6 inches) 220 pages, (CSIP, 2018), ISBN 978 1726407847 (Also an E-Book)

GUIDE TO WHITSTABLE AND ITS SURROUNDINGS 1876 (Illustrated), (with W J Cox) Soft Cover, 230mm x 150mm, (9 x 6 inches) 103 pages, (Independently Published, 2019), ISBN 9781794180987 (Also an E-Book)

Books are available from True Treasure Books online at http://www.truetreasurebooks.net and your favourite online and offline retailers.

ABOUT THE AUTHOR

David Villanueva has been researching local and family history for over 40 years. In 1972, the chance gift of a book entitled: *A Fortune Under Your Feet*, inspired David to buy a metal detector to hunt for the coins he liked to collect. Although the machine wailed like a Banshee and struggled to find an old penny buried more than a couple of inches deep, it did actually work and David became hooked on metal detecting.

The key to making good finds with a metal detector is research and having a love of history, David honed his research skills to great effect. As a result, David became passionate about Manor Houses and shares his passion in this book.

David has written over fifteen books (which include titles on research, family and local history) and has had more than two dozen articles published in British magazines.

Connect with me online: http://www.truetreasurebooks.net